Panzer in the Gunsigh

German AFVs and Artillery in the ETO 1944-45 in US Army Photos

Text and Color Plates by Steven J. Zaloga

We welcome authors who can help
expand our range of books. If you
would like to submit material,
please feel free to contact us.

We are always on the look-out for new,
unpublished photos for this series.
If you have photos or slides or
information you feel may be useful to
future volumes, please send them to us
for possible future publication.
Full photo credits will be given upon
publication.

ISBN 962-361-109-9
printed in Hong Kong

This book is a companion to the previous title in this series. This new volume takes a somewhat different approach to the subject. While the first volume was based primarily on Signal Corps photographs of German AFVs, the current volume is heavily based on photos taken by technical intelligence teams. During World War II, the US Army deployed an Ordnance Technical Intelligence Section with the headquarters of Com Z, European Theater of Operations, US Army (ETOUSA) to collect information on enemy equipment. This unit is probably better known for its work on securing German missile technology at the end of the war, but it was active from June 1944 through the final campaigns in May 1945. This unit cooperated in these endeavors with their counterparts in British technical intelligence, and some of the vehicles seen in these pages were actually captured by British units and then inspected by the US teams.

In general, these teams did not focus on well-known types such as the Panther or PzKpfw IV, but instead kept an eye out for new types or for unusual variations of known types. The focus of the technical intelligence teams was two-fold: in part to keep abreast of threat posed by the latest German weaponry, and secondly to examine German technology that might have applications in future US weapons development. Most of these photos come from internal reports that were sent to other ordnance agencies, though some reports were used more broadly in unclassified technical intelligence journals. The photos taken by these teams were generally not of the high quality of photos taken by Signal Corps units. The Signal Corps units were professional photographers equipped with professional press cameras, especially the Graflex Speed Graphic 4x5 inch camera, and had access to professional dark-rooms for film processing. The ordnance teams were seldom professionally trained in camera use, used small cameras, such as 35mm cameras, and had their film processed where ever possible, often in less than ideal circumstances. This is apparent on some of the photos here. In spite of the lower technical quality of some of these photos, they remain of special interest to AFV modelers since they often cover obscure subjects, and provide detailed technical views seldom seen in the Signal Corps photos. Although some of these photos have appeared in print in the past, the photos here were digitally copied from original prints in the National Archives and processed using Adobe Photoshop and Extensis Intellihance software to provide the highest quality possible.

Late War German Weapons

German AFVs taking part in the final campaigns of World War II seem to hold a special fascination with modelers. The focus here is on this period of the war. To add a fresh look to this well-covered subject, some lesser known subjects are covered in this book. For example, the Kingtiger heavy tank has been the subject of dozens of books and articles and it is very difficult to find new photos on this subject. So this book takes a different slant, and provides a detailed look at the Culemeyer trailer used to move the Kingtiger. Some of the other lesser known, late war types are also examined.

One area not well covered in published accounts is German artillery. For US tank units, the threat of German anti-tank artillery was of equal or greater concern than German panzer. The technical intelligence teams paid special attention to new German anti-tank guns. The focus here is in two particular areas: the legendary 88mm gun, and the lesser known late-war anti-tank guns. The photos here are intended to provide a sampling of the types of 88mm guns encountered by the US Army in 1944-45. Although the 88mm FlaK 36 and FlaK 37 are perhaps the best-known types, other types such as the PaK 43/41 and PaK 43 were also encountered.

Special attention is provided here to the war's most powerful but most mysterious anti-tank guns, the 128mm guns. Some improvised 128mm guns based on surplus guns from the Jagdtiger program actually saw combat in the final weeks of the war. In addition, the Wehrmacht was developing a new 128mm gun which might have entered service in the summer of 1945 and both competitors in this program are depicted here.

Another aspect of German anti-tank defense which has largely escaped attention among AFV hobbyists is the Rhine PaK Front. In the final months of the war, the German defense industry was approaching collapse. The Rhine river was the last major geographic barrier in the West protecting the German industrial heartland from American and British assault. A number of German ordnance plants had manufactured AFV guns including 50mm, 75mm and 88mm guns, but were either unable to deliver them, or the tank assembly plants were unable to complete the intended vehicles. As a result, early in 1945 the ordnance plants were instructed to manufacture elementary static mounts for these AFV weapons so that they could be employed to create an anti-tank defense belt along the Rhine, and especially along the autobahn. These weapons are shown here in detail for the first time, though they are often mentioned in US combat accounts of the time.

Another curious weapon depicted here in detail for the first time is the Flakwerfer 44 Föhngeräte (Storm-weapon). This was one of the few German secret weapons which actually reached combat service in 1945, yet it is largely unknown. A battalion of these was deployed along the Rhine in the spring of 1945, and took part in the fighting at the Remagen bridge. Besides posing a threat to Allied aircraft, they were also apparently used against Allied ground targets as a dual-purpose weapon. German Flak batteries posed a special worry to US Army tank units as they plunged deeper into the German industrial heartland in the Ruhr. These industrial facilities were usually protected by belts of 88mm, 105mm and 128mm Flak guns, which were a serious hazard when used in the direct-fire anti-tank mode. A number of these positions are shown here.

Late War Panzer

One of the alternative forms of protective skirts for the Pz.Kpfw. IV were the wire mesh shields sometimes nicknamed Thoma shields.

US technical intelligence was intrigued by the idea of the screen skirts, and this is a close-up photo taken to show the type of wire mesh used.

A Panther knocked out in the winter of 1944-45 in an unknown location.

Another detail view of the screen skirts, this time showing the mounting attachments.

A pair of Panther Ausf. G knocked out in the fighting in the winter of 1944-45.

A Panther Ausf. G of the 11th Panzer Division knocked out during fighting with the US 1st Infantry Division near Fernegierscheid during the failed counter-attacks against the Remagen bridgehead which began on 23 March 1945.

A Panther Ausf. G tank lies burned out in the streets of Haiger on 29 March 1945 after having been knocked out by a tank from the 750th Tank Battalion while attacking the 104th Division. This was part of the attempt Bayerlein's 53rd Corps to strike the flank of US Army's envelopment of the Ruhr pocket.

This Panther Ausf. G and Hetzer were sent back to the US for technical evaluation and later expended as range targets.

While hardly qualifying as a "late-war panzer" the US Army encountered increasing numbers of training tanks during the final fighting in Germany. This is a Panzer-Attrappen training tank built on an Opel P4 chassis of the type used in the early 1930s to train tank troops prior to the German re-militarization. It was still in use for training when captured by the US Army near Beyreuth in late April 1945.

Bergepanzer

This Bergepanther was captured in the Ardennes by the US First Army during the Battle of the Bulge and was inspected in the early winter of 1945. In this view, the small jib crane is erected.

A view of the same Bergepanther from the left rear side with the jib crane dismantled.

A detail view into the winch compartment under the work platform.

Another detail view of the Bergepanther winch compartment, this time looking in from the front.

A rear view of the Bergepanther showing the stabilizing spade folded up in travel position as well as the heavy duty towing pintle.

A detail view of the work platform with various tow hooks and tools on display. A forced air heater on skids is stowed on the rear of the platform.

Kingtiger

This Kingtiger was knocked out during fighting near Dornholzhausen on 12 April 1945 by the US First Army during the Ruhr fighting.

A Signal Corps photographer looks at the battle damage suffered by a Kingtiger of s.Pz.Abt. 507 of Panzergruppe Hudel knocked out during the fighting in Osterode on 12 April 1945.

Moving the Kingtiger by road was a daunting proposition and the usual Wehrmacht method was to use the 68-tonne Culemeyer trailer. This trailer had an unloaded weight of 23 tonnes.

This view shows the Culemeyer in the empty travel mode with the ramps stowed on the rear. The Culemeyer trailers were a standard pre-war design used originally for moving railroad equipment.

A rear view of the Culemeyer trailer with the ramps stowed.

This is a detail shot of the rear suspension bogies. The trailer consisted of two sets of articulated bogies, each with three sets of wheels.

Another view of the Culemeyer trailer showing the method that the first and last axle assemblies connected to the center set.

A detail view of one of the road-wheels.

A close-up showing the steering linkage that was used to coordinate the steering between the bogie assemblies.

A close-up view of the draw-bar for towing the Culemeyer. The usual Wehrmacht tractor for this trailer was the Sd.Kfz. 9 half-track or the commercial Kaelble tractor.

A crew preparing the Culemeyer trailer for loading.

The Culemeyer trailer in the loading mode with the rear ramp in place.

A close-up showing the ramp extended for loading.

A US Army crew from the 463rd Ordnance Evacuation Battalion recovers a Kingtiger on board the Culemeyer trailer. This particular tank is the well-known "332" from s.Pz.Abt. 501 attached to Kampfgruppe Peiper during the Battle of the Bulge and currently preserved at the Patton Museum at Fort Knox.

A view of the Kingtiger being driven up the rear ramp.

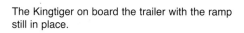

The Kingtiger on board the trailer with the ramp still in place.

A view of the rear of the trailer with the Kingtiger in place.

Late War Assault Guns and Tank Destroyers

The initial version of the Jagdpanzer IV was armed with the shorter L/48 gun and was not as commonly seen in the ETO as the later type with the L/70 gun. This one is seen in Normandy in the summer of 1944 being towed off a road by a M4 tank.

This is one of the first Panzer IV/70(V) captured in the autumn of 1944, chassis 340756. This version was actually intended as a tank substitute rather than a tank destroyer, being issued in lieu of the normal Pz.Kpfw. IV tank. It is from one of the earlier production batches, still finished with zimmerit.

An interior view of the fighting compartment of a Panzer IV/70(V) "Kunigunde".

One of the less common assault guns was the StuG IV and this one is seen being recovered by a US Army M32 tank recovery vehicle. It has suffered an internal explosion which removed the roof and much of the engine deck.

Another example of a StuG IV, knocked out near Helfengerhoff by the 776th Tank Destroyer Battalion on 9 March 1945. The nickname on the barrel is "Kunigunde".

A Panzer IV/70(A) knocked out in Mittewihr during the fighting in Alsace in late January 1945.

Steyr proposed an inexpensive tank destroyer mating the PaK 40 75mm gun to the Raupenshlepper Ost and these entered service in 1944.

A side view of a captured Raupenshlepper Ost (Sf) showing the armored carb and exposed rear gun mounting. This type was not widely encountered by the US Army in the ETO and this example may have been found at a depot or proving ground.

15

An overhead view of a 75mm Raupenshlepper Ost (Sf) with the side panels folded down.

An overhead view of the Raupenshlepper Ost (Sf). As will be noticed, the panels on the armored cab could be folded down over the opening to protect the driving compartment from blast when firing the gun over the front.

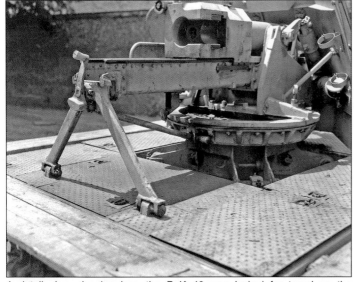

A detail view showing how the PaK 40 was locked for travel on the Raupenshlepper Ost (Sf).

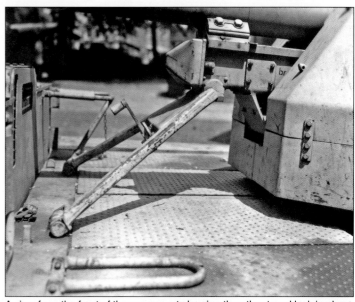

A view from the front of the gun mount showing the other travel lock in place.

A more commonly encountered tank destroyer in the winter of 1944-45 was the Sd.Kfz. 251/22 which mounted the 75mm PaK 40 on the standard army half-track. This particular vehicle belonged to the 11th Panzer Division.

Another view of the Sd.Kfz. 251/22. The 11th Panzer Division insignia can be seen on the hull rear.

A view into the fighting compartment of the Sd.Kfz. 251/22 showing the mounting for the PaK 40 and the crawl-space into the driving compartment.

An overhead view of the Sd.Kfz. 251/22 showing the PaK 40 mounting. Notice the spare ammunition to the left of the gun in the usual transport tubes.

Beutepanzer

The Wehrmacht made some combat use of the captured French Char B1bis in the anti-partisan role on the Russian front, but it was less commonly encountered in the West. However, some were used in a coastal defense role. This particular example was used for static beach defense in the Dieppe area where it was captured by Canadian troops. (NAC PA143907)

A close-up of this heavily camouflaged Char B1bis near Dieppe with a protective cover over its main 75mm gun in the hull. (NAC PA143908)

This particular example of the Leichter Schützenpanzerwagen U304(f) differs from the more common style in that it is fully enclosed. This was done since this particular vehicle was used as a radio command vehicle for three tactical radios.

The Wehrmacht made frequent use of captured equipment, especially French motor transport equipment. In 1943, some French Unic Kegresse P107 half-tracks were armored and this particular example was captured by Patton's Third Army in March 1945 during the Saar campaign.

This rear view shows the tactical markings of the vehicle which appears to indicate a heavy self-propelled artillery battalion.

Reconnaissance Vehicles

A Sd.Kfz. 250/9 captured by the US Fifth Army during the Anzio fighting and put back into use. Behind it is a Panther of 1/Pz.Rgt. 4.

This Sd.Kfz. 250/9 was captured in France in 1944 from the 116th Panzer Division and is on the later Neu chassis with the Hangelafette gun mount.

A useful rear view of the Sd.Kfz. 250/9 of the 116th Panzer Division showing the standard divisional leaping greyhound insignia as well as the tactical insignia for a half-track reconnaissance unit. There is also an interesting unit insignia in the shield to the right.

A detail view looking down into the turret showing the mounting tray for the 20mm gun as well as the co-axial machine gun.

A view of the front of the turret with the anti-grenade screen in place. The 20mm KwK 38 gun is missing.

A close-up of the front interior of the Hangelafette 38 mounting with the grenade screens opened.

A detail view of the right side of the Hangelafette 38 mounting in the Sd.Kfz. 250/9.

Another attempt to field a tracked reconnaissance vehicle was the Aufklärer Pz.Kpfw. 38(t) which placed the 20mm Hangelafette 38 turret on the Czechoslovak 38(t) chassis.

This front view shows the slightly raised superstructure of this variant and the plated-over machine gun port.

21

Another overhead view of the reconnaissance tank version of the Pz.Kpfw. 38(t) of which some 50 were converted in February-March 1944.

This Sd.Kfz. 234/1 was briefly examined by US First Army intelligence in February 1945 following the Battle of the Bulge and a few photos taken of its key features. This view of the interior of the Sd.Kfz. 234/1 turret showing the 20mm cannon main armament.

A detail view into the turret of the Sd.Kfz. 234/1 showing the rear of the breech.

This Sd.Kfz. 234/2 was examined by US intelligence officers in March 1945 after it had been captured by the British from 1./Pz.Aufkl.Abt. 2. The vehicle license number is WH-1542940, tactical number "1111", and the vehicle was subsequently shipped to Britain for further exploitation.

The Sd.Kfz. 234/2 was first encountered in the summer of 1944 and a few badly damaged examples were inspected by Allied intelligence such as this one in France.

A view of the left side shows extensive damage including the complete lack of side fenders.

This close-up of the roof of "1111" shows the commander's T.Rbl.3 observation periscope to the left, as well as the empty smoke mortar mountings.

An engine interior view from a Sd.Kfz. 234/2 examined in France in 1944.

A view into the engine compartment showing the Tatra V-12 diesel engine from vehicle "1111".

A close-up of the rear hatch area showing the engine fan as well as the center hub of the spare rear tire which has burned away.

An interior view of the right front side of the turret interior showing the commander's T.Rbl.F.3 periscopic observation periscope.

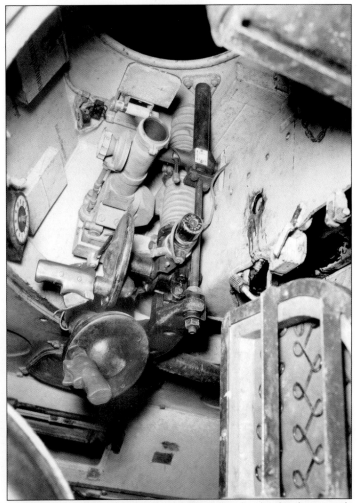

An interior view of the left front side of the turret interior showing the gunner's station with the associated controls and T.Z.F.4b telescopic sight.

This Sd.Kfz. 234 is fitted with the 20mm Schwebelafette mounting and it is not clear if this was a field improvisation or a prototype.

This overhead view show the 20mm turret mount of this vehicle, a weapon also seen on the Sd.Kfz. 251/17. This vehicle was apparently captured in Czechoslovakia and may have served with the 20th Panzer Division.

Halftracks

In December 1944, the 350th Ordnance Battalion mounted a 4.5 inch Calliope multiple rocket launcher on a captured Sd.Kfz. 251 half-track.

This shows the improvised Sd.Kfz. 251 Calliope launcher being fired in Belgium on 15 December 1944.

One of the first encounters with the late-production Sd.Kfz. 251/17 was during the Battle of the Bulge when a kampfgruppe of the Führer-Grenadier-Brigade attacked the US 80th Division near Heiderscheid on Christmas Eve 1944, losing at least two Sd.Kfz. 251 and several StuG III assault guns.

Another example of a Sd.Kfz. 251/17 with 20mm Schwebelafette in this case captured by the 6th Armored Division near Kalborn, Luxembourg in early February 1945. The gun is missing on this example, but this photo provides a view of the small shield around the gun.

This is a close-up of the 20mm Schwebelafette, though the gun shield has been knocked out.

The final version of the Sd.Kfz. 251/17 had a 20mm autocannon in a small turret mount sometimes called the Schwebelafette. This particular example was captured in the Saar by Patton's Third Army.

The Schwere Wehrmacht Schlepper (sWS) was a relatively late transport half-track which entered service in 1944. This particular example was being used impressed into US service by a unit of Patton's Third Army.

This sWS was knocked out in the Saar by Patton's Third Army and was being used to transport artillery ammunition.

A rear detail view of the sWS in US service.

A detail view of the tracked rear suspension of the sWS. This half-track used conventional wide dry pin track more similar to German tank track than typical half-track track.

An armored cab was introduced for the sWS in 1944, primarily used for self-propelled anti-aircraft guns. However, this Luftwaffe vehicle inspected in April 1945 lacks the weapon.

This detail shot of the rear-bed of the armored sWS shows that it has the fittings for carrying an anti-aircraft gun, typically the 37mm FlaK 43.

The Sd.Kfz. 7 was widely used in a number of specialized roles. This particular example had a special stowage frame on the rear bed used for carrying maintenance and repair tools.

A detail shot of the interior of the armored sWS cab.

Flakpanzer

The Flakpanzer 38(t) was the most common encountered anti-aircraft tank in the Normandy campaign in the summer of 1944.

This rear detail view shows the muffler and extended rear compartment of the Flakpanzer 38(t).

This is a detail view of the interior of a Flakpanzer 38(t) where the FlaK 38 gun mount has been removed, showing the baseplate for the weapon.

This detail view shows a damaged FlaK 38 20mm anti-aircraft gun mounting in a Flakpanzer 38(t).

The Möbelwagen mated the 37mm FlaK 43 with the Pz.Kpfw. IV chassis and was first encountered by the US Army in Normandy in June 1944. This example has the side panels folded down.

This detail view shows the interior of the fighting compartment with folding side panels erected. The spare barrel stowage is evident on the right wall.

A detail view of the FlaK 43 37mm gun mount on the Möbelwagen.

A close-up of the breech area of the 37mm FlaK 43 on the Möbelwagen.

Sd.Kfz. 234/2, 2nd Panzer Division, Normandy, July 1944

This Puma armored car of the 2nd Panzer Division's reconnaissance battalion was finished in the typical summer 1944 scheme. It was delivered to the unit in overall RAL 7028 dark yellow and the unit then added an irregular pattern of RAL 6003 olive green and RAL 8017 brown over this finish using a spray-gun. The vehicle's tactical number is unusual in that the platoon number was repeated in white on the fenders.

Hotchkiss 10.5cm leFH 18 auf Geschützwagen 38H(f), Sturmgeschütz-Abteilung 200, 21st Panzer Division, Normandy, June 1944

The so-called "Becker conversions" were widely used in the 21st Panzer Division in Normandy. They received the standard Wehrmacht finish of RAL 7028 dark yellow with a sprayed pattern of RAL 6003 olive green and RAL 8017 brown. In this case, the pattern is somewhat more elaborate than was usually the case with the chocolate brown color being used to break-up the other colors. This unit does not appear to have regularly used tactical numbers or other markings. An added form of camouflage was the provision of some netting on the super-structure front for the attachment of foliage, and these vehicles were usually covered with foliage during the Normandy fighting to hide from the dreaded Allied fighter-bombers.

Marder III, 1.Kp/Pz.Jg.Abt. 346, 346th Infantry Division, Netherlands, September 1944
This Marder III is finished in the usual scheme of RAL 7028 dark yellow with patches of RAL 6003 olive green edged in RAL 8017 brown. The scheme is unusually neat compared to the more slap-dash style seen commonly in Normandy. The markings include the usual tactical number and cross.

Panther-Befehlswagen Ausf. G, Panzer Brigade 105, Belgium, September 1944
This was the command tank of the brigade adjutant, knocked out in fighting with the US Army near Eynatten on the German frontier on 12 September 1944. The pattern is similar to other summer 1944 schemes seen here, a cloud pattern of RAL 6003 olive green patches surrounded with a thin border of RAL 8017 brown over the usual RAL 7028 dark yellow base color.

Jagdpanzer 38, Unit Unknown, Army Group B, 1944

This was one of the first Hetzers captured by the Allies on the Western Front and is typical of the early production batches. The first production batch of Hetzers appeared in overall RAL 7028 dark yellow. A number of Hetzers appeared in this type of scheme in the late summer of 1944 on both the Western Front and the Russian Front, which suggests that the scheme was either applied at the factory or at a depot prior to issuance to troops. The small black tactical numbers are not typical of German markings practice at this time.

Jagdpanzer 38, Unit Unknown, Army Group G, Alsace, December 1944

The late summer production run of Hetzers at the BMM plant in occupied Czechoslovakia was finished in a more elaborate scheme than the early batches consisting of overall RAL 7028 dark yellow, but heavily covered with RAL 6003 olive green and patches of RAL 8017 brown. The style of application suggests that it was applied using an airbrush fitted with a circular stencil attachment. To further break up the pattern, an overspray was added, also using a special template with moveable circular masks, to create a dappled "ambush" pattern in RAL 7028 dark yellow over the darker colors.

Sd.Kfz. 215/17, Führer-Grenadier-Brigade, Luxembourg, December 1944
This vehicle was part of the kampfgruppe that attacked the US 80th Division during the Battle of the Bulge on Christmas Eve. The finish is RAL 7028 dark yellow with bands of RAL 6003 olive green and RAL 8017 brown covering most of the surface, but heavily over-painted with whitewash. Whitewash was not common this early in the Ardennes fighting, as heavy snow had only begun to fall two days earlier on 22 December 1944.

Jagdpanzer 38, Unit Unknown, 15th Army, Kesternich, Germany, January 1945
This Hetzer served with a volksgrenadier division during the fighting in the Eifel in January 1945 following the end of the Battle of the Bulge. Whitewash finishes were not especially common on German AFVs, but were sometimes seen as in this case.

Sd.Kfz. 251/9, 1/504 Parachute Infantry Regiment, 82nd Airborne Division, Belgium, January 1945

The 1st Battalion of the 504th Parachute Infantry Regiment captured two of these assault guns from the 1st SS Panzer Division before Christmas in December 1944. They were prominently marking with crude white crosses on all surfaces to prevent friendly fire incidents. They were used throughout the Battle of the Bulge.

Flammpanzer 38, Army Group G, Alsace, February 1945

Only 20 of these flamethrower Hetzers were built, equipping two companies. This one was knocked out during Operation Nordwind in Alsace while supporting the 17th SS Panzer Grenadier Division. The scheme is 7028 dark yellow with bands of RAL 6003 olive green and RAL 8017 brown covering most of the surface, and was probably factory applied. The tactical number is unusual due to its "S" prefix.

Sd.Kfz. 251/17, Army Group G, Saar-Palatinate, March 1945
This fire support vehicle was captured by Patton's Third Army in the Saar. It is painted in 7028 dark yellow with bands of RAL 6003 olive green and RAL 8017 brown. This is probably a factory finish, and there are a number of photos in varied locations showing various types of Sd.Kfz. 251 with a very similar pattern.

Sd.Kfz. 234/2, Army Group B, Germany 1945
This Puma is finished in the usual scheme of RAL 7028 dark yellow with sprayed bands of RAL 6003 olive green and RAL 8017 brown. The tactical numbers are the reduced-visibility late war style of black outlines. This particular vehicle was later sent back to the United States for trials.

M4A3 (76mm), SS Panzer Brigade Westfalen, Paderborn, Germany, April 1945
During the attempts to stop the US breakout from the Remagen bridgehead, the training school near Paderborn formed an improvised brigade to attack the advancing 3rd Armored Division. At one point during the fighting for the city, the brigade used a captured M4A3 (76mm) hastily repainted with a prominent swastika. It was probably captured from the 3rd Armored Division, and has a Company B name "Battlin' Boys" along with a standard shipping code on the side in black, and is finished in the standard First Army pattern of black over olive drab.

Kingtiger, s.Pz.Abt. 507, Panzergruppe Hudel, Germany, April 1945
This Kingtiger was one of a number provided to s.Pz.Abt. 507 before the unit was hastily dispatched towards Remagen as part of the improvised Panzergruppe Hudel, intended to crush the US bridgehead after the capture of the Ludendorff bridge. It is finished in the late factory scheme of overall RAL 6003 olive green with small bands of RAL 7028 dark yellow. The edges of both colors have small splotches of the opposite color to break up the pattern, a relatively late example of "ambush" camouflage. The unit did not have time to apply tactical markings and photos of their tanks from this period show no tactical numbers.

Sd.Kfz. 234/2, 1st SS Panzer Division, Czechoslovakia, May 1945

This Puma probably belonged to the 1st SS Panzer Division and was surrendered at the end of the war in Czechoslovakia. The scheme is the usual 7028 dark yellow with bands of RAL 6003 olive green and RAL 8017 brown. The markings are a bit odd in that the lead number is trimmed in white but the other two remained without white trim. This is probably due to the fact that the second and third numbers were over-painted at some stage.

Sd.Kfz. 234, 20th Panzer Division, Czechoslovakia, May 1945

This Sd.Kfz. 234 was captured in Czechoslovakia in May 1945 and apparently served with the 20th Panzer Division. It consists of a Sd.Kfz. 234/3 with the usual 75mm howitzer removed, the fighting compartment cut down and a 20mm Schwebelafette added in its place. The color scheme suggests that this was an improvisation as the Schwebelafette appears to be finished in red primer, the side armor in a freshly re-painted finish, and the rest of the vehicle in a very battered finish.

A front view of the Sd.Kfz. 161/3 Möbelwagen.

A side view of the Möbelwagen with the side panels folded down.

Although not the best quality, this photo provides a rare view of a Möbelwagen with a tactical insignia, the number "23" on the side panels.

41

The Wirblewind 20mm FlaK 38-Vierling was first issued in the summer of 1944 for defense of panzer units against air attack, and only 122 were completed. This one was probably lost in the Ardennes, and it was inspected by a US First Army team in March 1945.

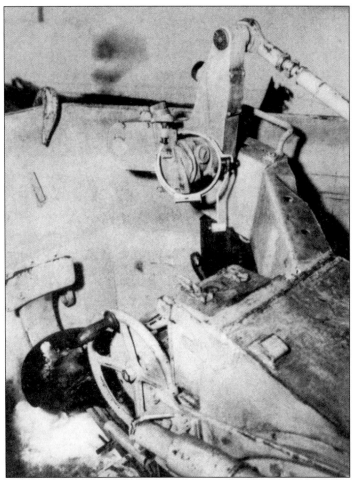

This detail view is looking towards the left rear of the turret, and shows the articulation for the gunner's sight.

This detail view looks down towards the front of the turret with the gun controls evident.

This detail view shows the interior of the armored cab on the Sd.Kfz. 7/1.

This view looks at the right rear wall of the turret showing the stowage of the ammunition magazines.

The Sd.Kfz. 7/1 mounted the 20mm FlaK 38 and this particular example shows the armored cab configuration. It was captured by Patton's Third Army and the markings appear to indicate a vehicle of the 3rd company of Pz.Jg.Abt. 256.

This detail view shows how the FlaK 38 outrigger was attached to the special floor mounts on the Sd.Kfz. 7/1.

This is a detail view of the front armored cab of a Sd.Kfz. 7/2.

The Sd.Kfz. 7/2 mounted the 37mm FlaK 36 and this example was captured by the Third Army in the Saar.

This detail view shows the method for attaching the FlaK 36 outriggers to the Sd.Kfz. 7/2 rear-bed.

US troops inspect a knocked out Sd.Kfz. 7/2 with a prominent hole through the front armor panel.

Self-propelled Artillery

The standard heavy self-propelled gun of the German panzer artillery units was the Sd.Kfz. 165 150mm Hummel. This example was captured by the US 69th Division near Wurzen on 25 April 1945.

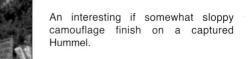

An interesting if somewhat sloppy camouflage finish on a captured Hummel.

This Hummel took a direct hit on the side armor plate, shattering it. It carries interesting tactical markings, the number "C35", which presumably refers to its battery.

A special version of the Hummel was fielded called the Geschützwagen III/IV fur Munition on a scale of two per battery of 6 Hummels. The Munitionsträger was essentially similar to the Hummel except for the lack of the gun and the plated over opening on the superstructure.

Another example of a Munitionsträger captured by the US Fifteenth Army in the Ruhr in 1945 from the front.

Another view of the same Munitionsträger from the rear showing the general configuration.

This interior view of the Munitionsträger shows the simple layout, lacking any specialized storage racks.

A Geschützwagen Tiger was planned to accommodate a variety of heavy artillery weapons, and the first assembled, the Gerät 809, was intended for the 170mm K72. A single pilot was in the final stages of construction in the spring of 1945 when it was captured by the US Army. This composite photo was created by US Army intelligence based on several photos taken inside the storage hanger where the vehicle was found.

This was the intended weapon for the Gerät 809, a derivative of the standard 170mm gun but with a carriage adapted for the new vehicle.

This is a close-up of the muzzle brake intended for the 170mm gun when used on the self-propelled mounting.

This front overhead shows the general configuration of the Gerät 809 in its storage hanger. It was powered by a Maybach HL230P30 engine mounted in the center of the chassis.

The enormous size of the 170mm gun meant that the rear fighting compartment of the Gerät 809 was substantial as seen from the members of the Allied intelligence team.

88mm Anti-tank and FlaK Guns

The 88mm gun earned its legendary reputation as an anti-tank weapon on many fronts, but was best known to the British for its role in the North African desert like the one seen here with numerous kill markings on its tube. This particular photo was later found by US troops in Tunisia.

The US Army first encountered the 88mm gun in Tunisia and this example with three kill rings on its barrel was photographed near Ferryville in Tunisia.

One of the less commonly encountered versions of the 88mm gun was the FlaK 41, a type usually reserved for Reich defense. This one captured near Cori, Italy in May 1944 following the Anzio break-out.

Most of the D-Day beaches had one or more 88mm PaK 43/41 anti-tank guns in H677 bunkers to provide enfilade fire along the beach. This example forced the core of the WN29 strongpoint near the harbor in Courseulles-sur-Mer and is seen several days after D-Day after Canadian troops had established an anti-aircraft position on top with 20mm cannon. (Ken Bell, NAC PA140856)

This 88mm PaK 43/41 was located in an H677 bunker on the eastern side of the Colleville draw in strongpoint WN61 at Omaha Beach on D-Day where it was knocked out by a M4 of the 741st Tank Battalion. It was pulled out of the bunker later when the fortification was converted to a medical aid station and is seen here overlooking a LCI on the beach. There were two 88mm guns on Omaha Beach, on opposite sides to cover the entire beach with enfilade fire.

One of the deadliest bunkers on Omaha Beach was this H677 armed with a 88mm PaK 43/41 in strongpoint WN72 near the Vierville draw, at the western side of the beach opposite the other bunker at WN61. This bunker was in the sector assaulted by the 116th Infantry Regiment and elements of the 2nd and 5th Ranger Battalions, made famous in the movie "Saving Private Ryan".

This view from the 88mm gun position of WN72 makes it clear why this 88mm gun was so effective on Omaha Beach on D-Day since it has a commanding view over the entire beach all the way east to the other H677 bunker in strongpoint WN61. It was finally knocked out around noon by close-range destroyer fire.

This camouflaged 88mm FlaK 37 was captured by the 82nd Airborne Division in Normandy after D-Day. The FlaK 37 can be distinguished from the earlier FlaK 36 by its improved fire controls on the right side as seen here.

This 88mm gun with the later pattern shield was photographed on 31 July 1944 during the Operation Cobra break-out from the Normandy beach-head.

So much German artillery was captured in France that an improvised field artillery brigade was organized by the US Army to exploit the captured guns and ammunition. This 88mm PaK 43 is being emplaced by the 733rd Field Artillery Battalion on 29 September 1944.

Another view of an 88mm PaK 43 of the US 733rd Field Artillery Battalion being deployed near Urcourt, France on 18 October 1944.

A pair of GIs examine an 88mm FlaK abandoned by the roadside near Grandvillers, France in October 1944.

US troops take a break near a captured 88mm PaK 43/41. This version of the 88mm gun used the carriage and limber of the standard 100mm gun/150mm howitzer.

A view of the PaK 43 after it was emplaced by the 733rd Field Artillery Battalion on 25 October 1944. Curiously enough, the battery used a captured and repainted Sd.Kfz. 251 Ausf. D as the prime mover for the gun.

An 88mm FlaK overrun near Metz during the fighting on 18 November 1944 in an improvised firing position, firing with the limbers in place and the outriggers down.

One of the US units converted to use German artillery was the 244th Field Artillery Battalion seen here firing an 88mm PaK 43/41 in support of the 6th Armored Division during the Battle of the Bulge on 21 December 1944.

Another example of an 88mm FlaK 41. This one has numerous aircraft kill markings on its side panel.

This 88mm PaK 43 was captured by the 14th Armored Division near Surburg with is barrel and shield heavily covered in foliage.

An 88mm FlaK being used for improvised anti-tank defense in Cologne and captured on 7 March 1945. There are two 88mm rounds still in the fuze setter on the left side of the trunnion.

An 88mm FlaK captured in Trier in March 1945 by the 10th Armored Division with the ground around it littered with spent ammunition casings.

An 88mm FlaK 37 being used by the 95th Armored Field Artillery Battalion of the 5th Armored Division near Moers, Germany on 11 March 1945. Visible in the background is a 75mm PaK 40 anti-tank gun, probably also being used to provide a bit of added firepower.

An 88mm FlaK 37 being used by the US Army's Battery B, 325th Field Artillery Battery near Jerdigen, Germany on 15 March 1945.

This 88mm gun with the later pattern shield was captured by the 771st Tank Battalion near Dulmen, Germany on 29 March 1945. It has a fairly intricate pattern of brown and green camouflage over the base dark yellow.

The 88mm FlaK was widely encountered by US tank units in Germany in March-April 1945 as they encountered the many air defense belts around German cities. This 88mm was knocked out by the 14th Armored Division near Hartheim, and one round can be seen still in position in the fuze setter on the left side of the gun trunnion.

Another view of the FlaK belt at Hartheim encountered by the 14th Armored Division with a pair of 88mm FlaK.

128mm Anti-tank Guns

This Jagdtiger (X7, 305058) was the first intact vehicle captured by US troops and so examined extensively by US First Army technical intelligence officers. It was commanded by Lt. Sepp Tarlach and served with the second platoon, 1./s.Pz.Jg.Abt. 512 of s.Panzergruppe Hudel, part of a scratch German force attempting to stop the US Army's exploitation of the Remagen bridgehead in late March 1945.

A front view of X7 showing the large folding travel lock. The 1.C marking is probably a US marking.

A side view of the X7 where it was abandoned in Obernephen.

A rear view of X7 showing the anti-aircraft mount for the MG42 in place.

A detail view of the MG42 mount on the rear engine deck.

An overhead view showing roof detail.

A view in the rear door showing the breech of the massive 128mm gun.

A detail view inside the fighting compartment showing the gun breech to the left, the recuperator above it, and the vehicle commander's seat.

A detail view showing the side ammunition stowage. The 128mm ammunition was the semi-fixed type with separate projectile and propellant casing.

This Jagdtiger, "131" of 1./s.Pz.Jg.Abt. 653 was knocked out on Heidelbergstrasse in Schwetzingen by a M4 medium tank of CCB/10th Armored Division which hit it twice on its thinner side armor. The other two Jadgtigers of the platoon were also lost that day, one after bogging down and the other after it shed a track while retreating from the town.

Since there were about 80 128mm guns built beyond those used in the Jagdtiger, there was an effort made in 1945 to hastily adapt these weapons as towed anti-tank guns. Two configurations were built, the Kanone 81/1 on French 155mm GPF carriages, and the Kanone 81/2 like the one here on Soviet ML-20 152mm gun-howitzer carriages.

A detail side view of a K81/2 128mm gun.

A detailed front view of the K81/2 128mm anti-tank gun.

A detailed rear view of a captured K81/2 128mm anti-tank gun.

Besides the carriage mounted 128mm anti-tank guns, a small number were also deployed on simple pedestal mounts on improvised cruciform bases as part of the Rhine PaK Front.

Although resembling the 88mm FlaK, this is in fact a 128mm FlaK 40 used for Reich air defense. This example from the unit defending the Hermann Göring Steel Works in Leuna fought a violent battle with the CCA/2nd Armored Division on 10 April 1945 before being outflanked and overrun. A single 128mm round is in the fuze setter.

Besides the improvised 128mm anti-tank guns, there was a program underway since 1944 to field a dual-purpose 128mm field/anti-tank gun. Two competitive designs were developed and this is the Krupp version of the 128mm PaK 44, also known as the PaK 80 and Kanone 44. This shows the weapon in the travel configuration.

This shows the Krupp version of the PaK 44 in the firing position with the cruciform platform lowered to the ground and outriggers deployed.

A detail view of the front carriage of the Krupp 128mm PaK 44.

The Rheinmetall 128mm PaK 44 had a somewhat more elaborate gun shield and a six-wheel carriage configuration.

A good study of the Rheinmetall 128mm PaK 44 in travel mode.

A front view of the Rheinmetall 128mm PaK 44 showing its elaborate front carriage.

A detail view of the Rheinmetall 128mm PaK 44 showing the breech area and rear of the gun-shields.

One of the rarest late-war German flak weapons was the Flakwerfer 44 Föhngeräte, (Storm-weapon). This was a mobile launcher which fired a salvo of thirty-five 73mm unguided rockets. This particular example belonged to the 900th Flak Training and Test Battalion stationed along the Rhine to defend bridges, in this case, the famous Ludendorff bridge at Remagen.

This shows an example of a Flakwerfer 44 in a static configuration and gives some idea of the size of the weapon.

Another view of a static Flakwerfer 44 named Marta.

This rear view of a static Flakwerfer 44 shows the operator's controls which were quite elementary, consisting of a simple sight and manual controls for elevating the rocket array.

A close up of the gunner's controls on the Flakwerfer 44.

A side view of the Flakwerfer 44 showing the rocket array.

A detail shot of the rocket launch array on the Flakwerfer 44.

Another view of the mobile towed Flakwerfer 44.

The Flakwerfer 44 also was issued in a mobile configuration as seen here on a small trailer, though in this case, the tires are missing.

Rhine PaK Front

During the defense of the Rhine in March 1945, a number of 50mm KwK 39 guns intended for the Sd.Kfz. 234/2 Puma armored car were hastily converted into fixed anti-tank guns. Note the different muzzle brake employed.

A front view of the Rhine KwK 39 50mm gun.

A detail view from the rear of the static KwK 39 50mm gun.

This detail shot shows the simple base adopted for the static version of the 75mm gun.

As in the case of the surplus 50mm guns, surplus KwK 75mm guns were also converted into static defense guns for the Rhine PaK Front.

A view of the right side of the gun shows the simple base-plate for the fixed 75mm gun.

A view of the gunner's controls of the fixed-site 75mm anti-tank gun for the Rhine PaK Front.

This is an example of a pedestal mounted KwK 40 75mm gun on a pedestal mount encountered by the US Army during the fighting along the Rhine in March-April 1945.

A number of PaK43/3 88mm guns intended for the Jagdpanther tank destroyer were also converted to static mounts like this emplacement.

This shows the baseplate of the 88mm gun of the Rhine PaK Front.

This rear view shows the method of attaching the gun trunnions to a traversing baseplate when used in the static defense mode.

The Rhine PaK Front 88mm gun was fitted with conventional artillery sights when used in this role including a range quadrant.